INTERPRETING
SIGN LANGUAGE

INTERPRETING SIGN LANGUAGE

BY LAURA GREENE AND
EVA BARASH DICKER

Franklin Watts
New York   London   Toronto
Sydney 1989

Library of Congress Cataloging-in-Publication Data

Greene, Laura.
Interpreting sign language / by Laura Greene and Eva Barash
Dicker.
p. cm.
Includex index.
Summary: Presents a history of sign language interpreting and
discusses how and where it is done, who does it, and the necessary
training.
ISBN 0-531-10773-6
1. Interpreters for the deaf—United States—Juvenile literature.
[1. Interpreters for the deaf. 2. Sign language.] I. Dicker, Eva
Barash. II. Title.
HV2402.G74 1989
362.4'283—dc20   89-31825
CIP
AC

CONTENTS

CHAPTER 1 A HISTORY OF SIGN LANGUAGE INTERPRETING

INTERPRET

As long as there are different languages, there will be problems for people who speak different languages to understand one another. Interpreters help solve these problems. They make communication among people easier. An interpreter is a person who knows two or more languages well and is able to translate one language into a different language. Most interpreters do this with spoken languages. A spoken language is a language based on sound. English, German, French, Russian, etc., are spoken (as well as written) languages. Thus, an interpreter might translate English into German or French into Russian.

Sign language interpreters, however, are different from foreign language interpreters. Sign language interpreters (we do not call them *translators*) change spoken language into gestural/visual languages and back again. A gestural/visual language is a language based on movement and sight. The

The signs that are illustrated alongside the text in this book, and instructions for forming the signs, may be found in the Sign Language Dictionary beginning on page 62. All the signs are illustrated from the viewer's perspective—that is, as the person watching the signs being formed sees them.

process of changing a sound language into a movement language requires special skills that oral language translators don't need. These unique skills include acting, pantomime, and an understanding of the special communication needs of the hearing impaired.

Sign language interpreters are needed because deaf people and hearing people communicate in different ways. Every sign language interpreter must be fluent in spoken English and either American Sign Language (ASL) or any of the various systems that put signs into English word order.

HELPERS AND PROTECTORS

Long before sign language interpreting became a profession, hearing people who understood deaf people helped them to communicate with the hearing population. They were neither paid for their work nor trained nor educated in any special way. These early interpreters were family members, church people, and teachers who knew both sign language and English. Sometimes their interpreting abilities were very good, but sometimes they were not. These "interpreters" cared a great deal about the people they tried to help. They thought of themselves as "protectors" of deaf people. They often acted like parents and treated deaf adults like children.

In addition to helping their deaf relatives and friends communicate, these interpreters often made decisions for them and gave them unasked-for advice on what to do, how to act, and what to buy. For example, when a deaf person wanted to move to a new house, the "helper" would often decide which house was best for the deaf person. Sometimes the decisions were good ones, but sometimes they were not. The more decisions hearing people made for deaf people, the fewer decisions deaf people made for themselves.

HOUSE

Deaf people usually appreciated the help they received, and hearing people felt good about helping. However, neither group fully realized that this kind of help made the hearing impaired more and more dependent upon the hearing. People came to think that those who could hear were

Sign language interpreters change spoken languages into gestural/visual languages and back again. At a Veteran's Day service, an interpreter changes President Ronald Reagan's address into sign language.

smarter and more capable than those who could not. Deaf parents with hearing children (and most deaf parents have hearing children) found themselves relying a great deal on their children for communication and decision making. In fact, they often expected their hearing children to play a major role in family decisions, such as which automobile to purchase or whether or not to take a vacation.

Psychologists, teachers, deaf people, and those professionals who worked with deaf people felt that something had to change. They knew that deaf parents sometimes gave their hearing children too much responsibility and that this was not good for either the children or their parents. They also knew that deaf people can be as intelligent as hearing people and need no special protection. Furthermore, they believed very strongly that deaf people had to have the right to make their own choices and their own mistakes. What deaf people did need, however, were trained interpreters who could help make it easier for them to communicate with the hearing world.

INTERPRETING BECOMES A PROFESSION

On June 14, 1964, at Ball State Teachers College in Muncie, Indiana, those who worked with the hearing impaired met at a historic meeting. It was an ordinary meeting until Edgar Lowell, director of the John Tracy Clinic, and Ralph Hoag, superintendent of the New York State School of the Deaf, got up to speak. The two men began making suggestions destined to change the way the hearing and the hearing impaired would relate to one another in the future. They were putting into words a dream many people shared— the dream of moving interpreting from the position of makeshift job, hobby, or voluntary service to the status of a profession. This was the birth of the National Registry of Interpreters and Translators.

Those attending the meeting at Ball State College broke up into small groups and discussed what skills interpreters would need to have, how interpreters ought to act, and how an interested person could pursue a career as an interpreter. The suggestions of Lowell, Hoag, and the others

WHO

READ

led to the development of standards for sign language interpreting. From this time on, sign language interpreting would no longer be only a voluntary activity for people who wanted to help the deaf. It would be a profession like other professions, with standard pay and a code of ethics. A code of ethics is a set of rules governing professional behavior. People in a given profession agree to abide by the rules and in the practice of their profession place the interests and needs of others above their own. You'll read more about this in Chapter Three. In time, the registry changed its name to the Registry of Interpreters for the Deaf, Inc. (RID), and became the single most important professional organization in the nation for the sign language interpreters.

A series of meetings followed the initial conference. Groups of people formed special committees that wrote the first handbook on interpreting and devised the original code of ethics. As a result of these meetings, hearing people as well as deaf people began to take the work of an interpreter seriously. They came to believe that the deaf had a right to skillful interpretation and that interpreting should not be a favor to be granted by a "helper" with inadequate skills. The work of RID enabled the hearing impaired to communicate with the hearing in a way that recognized the abilities, intelligence, and independence of the deaf.

It was not long after the Ball State conference that New York University and other colleges throughout the United States began to teach people how to become interpreters. Many members of deaf families attended those first training classes. Soon people began calling themselves sign language interpreters and began insisting on getting paid for their work.

At first, the deaf community was delighted to have professional help. It soon became clear, however, that although some interpreters were highly skilled, many others were not. In other words, some people who called themselves interpreters made many mistakes, had trouble understanding deaf clients, or did not follow the established code of ethics. The deaf community began to complain.

NATIONAL CERTIFICATION BEGINS

In 1972, the Registry of Interpreters for the Deaf decided that there ought to be a national certification program that separated skilled professional interpreters from unskilled ones or merely interested helpers. They agreed, therefore, to hold a national test to identify the highly skilled. Those who passed the test would receive certification and the privilege of calling themselves professional interpreters. Those who failed would need to improve their skills before earning certification. The first national evaluation took place in Memphis, Tennessee, in 1972. Almost every state in the United States sent a national representative for RID evaluation. The states chose their representatives very carefully, because those who passed would be given an important responsibility. They would form their own state's evaluation teams, which would, in turn, be responsible for evaluating the next generation of interpreters.

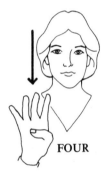

FOUR

At this national evaluation, RID issued four types of certificates. Hearing people were eligible to earn up to three of them, and deaf people were eligible for one. Employers soon began paying interpreters wages based on the ability and skills indicated by RID certification.

THREE

Eventually, RID began to provide opportunities for interpreters to become even more specialized within the profession. For example, RID began to offer training workshops and evaluations to those who wanted to learn more about interpreting in the specialized fields of law, theater, education, medicine, and mental health.

DEMAND FOR MORE INTERPRETERS

In the 1960s and 1970s, the U.S. government passed laws that helped to set up an ever-increasing demand for interpreters. Congress passed these laws partly in response to pressure from thousands of hearing-impaired citizens who believed they were unable to work to their full potential. They felt that they had less opportunity to advance because of the communication problem.

As a result of the new federal laws, additional specialized technical schools and advanced training programs became open to the hearing impaired all over the United States. New programs were designed to meet their needs. Most of these programs were started in vocational and technical schools originally set up for hearing people. Everyone hoped that hearing-impaired students would now be able to learn skills that would prepare them for jobs they had only dreamed of before. The problems, however, were not all solved. For example, the teachers in the vocational and technical schools did not know sign language. Thus, hearing-impaired students could not always understand what the teachers were saying. The schools, therefore, had to hire interpreters, and the need for interpreters grew. This special support made things better for the hearing impaired. However, there was still much room for improvement.

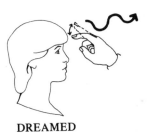

DREAMED

THE VOCATIONAL REHABILITATION ACT OF 1973

In 1973, the U.S. Congress passed the Vocational Rehabilitation Act, nicknamed the "Civil Rights for the Handicapped Act." This law would have a great impact on the entire country. Section 504 was particularly important, for it stated that schools, workplaces, and all agencies that received money from the federal government had to give handicapped people the same educational and employment opportunities that they gave nonhandicapped people.

For the physically disabled, it meant such things as wider doors, lowered drinking fountains, and wheelchair ramps. For the blind, it meant elevator information in Braille, tape-recorded lectures, and readers. For the hearing impaired, it meant accessible communication for most deaf individuals. The most effective way to accomplish accessible communication was through the use of an interpreter. Thus, by interpretation of the law, any program receiving federal funds would have to provide interpreter services. Such services would enable the hearing impaired to participate in programs that were never before open to them. All handicapped people looked forward to the equal treatment required by law and the new opportunities that would result from it.

BLIND

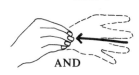

AND

THE CONSORTIUM The Vocational Rehabilitation Act of 1973 was a good law, but it soon became clear to those who had to hire interpreters that there was a serious shortage of skilled people. There were simply not enough trained interpreters available to help all those who needed them. The demand for interpreters continued to increase as more and more deaf *and* hearing people discovered how much easier communication became with the help of an interpreter.

Some deaf individuals contacted their legislators about the problem. The U.S. government responded by encouraging the opening of more schools and programs to train interpreters. They began by giving funds to six schools: the St. Paul Technical Vocational Institute (TVI) in Minnesota, the Seattle Community College (SCC) in Washington State, the California State University at Northridge (CSUN), the University of Tennessee (UT), Gallaudet College in Washington, D.C., and New York University (NYU). These schools established training centers and became known as the National Interpreter Training Consortium (NITC). The consortium helped nearby states start interpreter-training programs. They also developed and shared training materials and curriculum suggestions.

MORE SCHOOLS ARE ESTABLISHED

MONEY

TEN

In 1980, the federal government passed legislation that would result in the setting up of a number of new interpreter-training programs in the United States. Over forty colleges and universities were interested in receiving the money. They submitted proposals, or plans, that explained the kinds of programs they intended to establish if they received the money. People who worked for the federal government read the proposals and selected ten of them to receive the money. The ten schools were scattered throughout the United States, and the newly established programs, along with smaller programs already in existence, began to advertise for students. Before long, the classrooms were filled. Some schools even had waiting lists.

There were many people eager to become interpreters. They came from all over the United States and from a

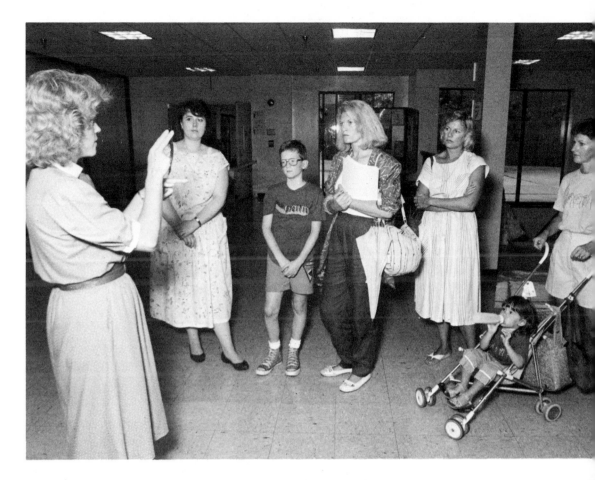

*Gallaudet College in Washington, D.C., is a center
for training interpreters. Here an interpreter leads
a group of deaf persons on a tour of the college.*

variety of economic and social backgrounds. Some students had deaf relatives or deaf friends; others did not know any deaf people. Some students knew sign language very well, and some were just beginning to learn signs. The one thing they all had in common was that they wanted to study the language and characteristics of the deaf community and learn the skills that would help them accurately pass information back and forth (receptively and expressively) between the hearing and the hearing impaired.

CHAPTER 2 SOURCE AND TARGET, CODES AND MODES

PRACTICE

A variety of students came to the newly established interpreter-training programs. Every one of them was drawn to sign language and wanted to learn more about deafness, deaf culture, and interpreting. All were eager to practice the skills that would help them become professional interpreters. These men and women were pioneers in a new field and looked forward to challenging opportunities.

Teachers in the interpreter-training programs taught their students about the causes, treatments, and meaning of deafness. They taught them what it meant to be a professional interpreter and how to abide by the code of ethics. They also taught them more about the history, vocabulary, and grammar of sign language.

The teachers expected their students to learn the specialized vocabulary of interpreting. This was important for their communications with one another on technical matters. Most professions have a technical vocabulary. A lawyer has to know what a *torte* and a *lien* are. A doctor has to know the difference between a *gland* and a *hormone*. Technical words can mean different things to different people. To an actor, the word *star* refers to the most important member of a theatrical production, but to an astronomer, the word *star* refers to a luminous, gaseous celestial body of great mass.

The word *interpret* has a different meaning to sign language interpreters than it does to artists or art critics. Artists may interpret life by painting pictures of what they think life is beneath surface appearances. Critics look at the pictures and interpret them by stating what the pictures mean to them. The critics may not view the pictures the same way the artists do. Yet all these individuals are interpreters.

To sign language interpreters, the word *interpret* means the act or process of translating one language into another so that everyone has the same understanding. These interpreters must know the vocabulary and the grammar of spoken English and either American Sign Language or a manual code for English (see p. 20), as well as the customs and the culture of the people who use them.

SOURCE TO TARGET

Interpreters must be fluent in both languages so that they can quickly translate one of them, called the *source language,* into the other, called the *target language.* Sometimes the source language is spoken English and the target language is ASL. Sometimes it works the opposite way. An interpreter must be fluent in both languages.

In order for interpreters to translate the source language into the target language, several things have to happen. First, interpreters must *see* ASL or *hear* spoken English. Second, they must think about what they saw or heard. This thinking stage we call *processing.* Third, interpreters must think about what the information means, and fourth, they must think about how to translate the source language into the target language without changing the sense, intent, or mood of the message. It is only after all this is done that the interpreter actually delivers the message either by sign or spoken word. Since this entire procedure needs to be done very quickly, interpreters need to be *bilingual.* A bilingual person is someone who has the ability to use two languages equally well.

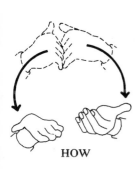

HOW

A ten-year-old student demonstrates sign language at an after-school signing class.

WHEN

Sometimes deaf people use a combination of ASL and English. This combination is often called Pidgin Sign English, or PSE. It is no one's native language. Instead, it is a language tool that hearing and deaf people frequently use when they talk to each other. This flexible combination of two languages contains a mixture of the vocabulary and the grammar of both English and ASL. When people actually communicate with each other, they can make it more like ASL or more like English. It depends upon the language skills of the individuals who are communicating. Interpreters must know how and when to use these combinations.

CODES AND TRANSLITERATION

Interpreters must also learn invented manual codes. An artificial code is not a language. It is a visible communication system in which signers use their hands to express themselves in English. We call such systems *manual codes for English* (MCE) or simply *Signed English*. There are several of these, and a professional interpreter must be aware of all of them and be flexible enough to apply them as needed.

THINKING

Unlike ASL, manual codes have no grammar of their own. Instead they follow the grammar and word order of the source language. Codes are used in *transliterating*. Transliterating is different from interpreting. It occurs when an interpreter listens to a spoken language such as English and then, almost without thinking, automatically picks a code with which to express the words in English word order. An interpreter must be able to transliterate as quickly as a speaker speaks. This enables the deaf person to immediately "see" the language as it is being spoken.

Let's look at an example. "Thorndike is eating snails" is a perfectly correct English sentence. An interpreter could sign the sentence in ASL this way:

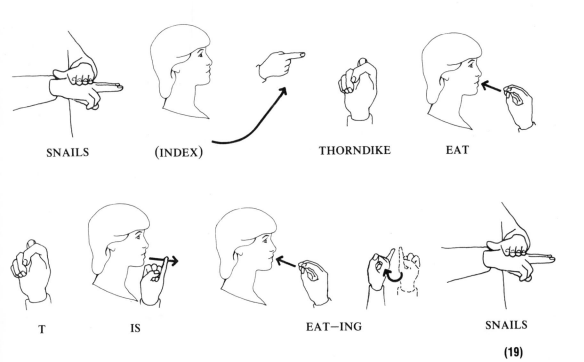

SNAILS   (INDEX)   THORNDIKE   EAT

T   IS   EAT—ING   SNAILS

Or, the interpreter could use a manual code for English and transliterate the sentence this way:

Notice that in MCE the interpreter has visually depicted each English word. In this particular manual code, the interpreter used a specific hand movement to indicate the -*ing* ending. Some codes regularly use movement to indicate word endings. In American Sign Language, however, once the tense has been established, it is only necessary to sign the main concept: "eat"

Let's look at another example: "Nimrod walks on a bridge while watching boats." An interpreter might sign the sentence in ASL this way:

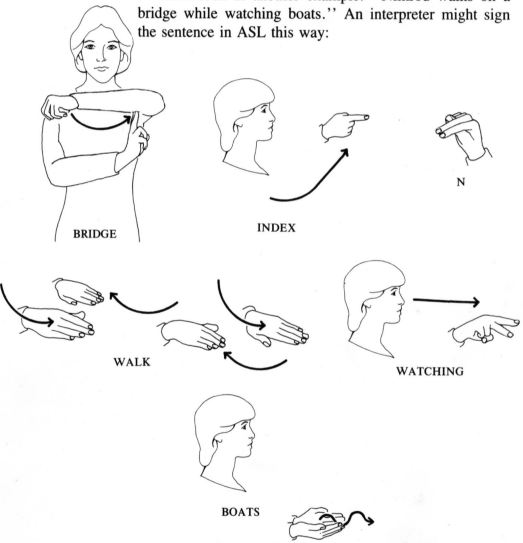

BRIDGE   INDEX   N

WALK   WATCHING

BOATS

The word order and the grammar are different from English word order and grammar. There is no tense marker because in an actual interpreting situation, the past tense would have been established in the context of a full message.

This same sentence could also be transliterated into a manually coded form of English.

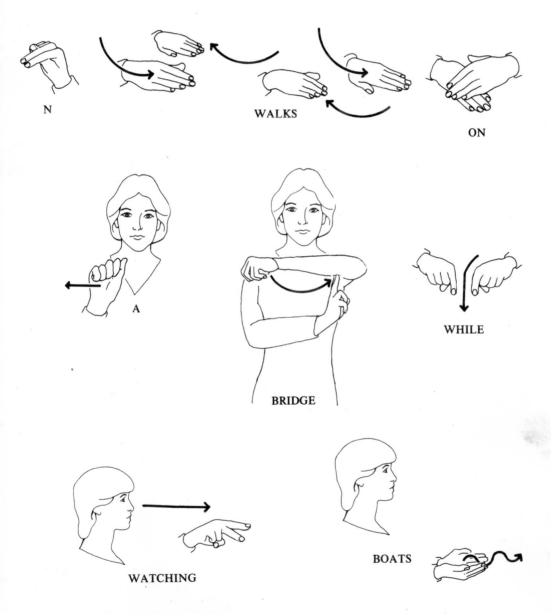

N   WALKS   ON

A   BRIDGE   WHILE

WATCHING   BOATS

Notice again that in the manual code the word order is identical to English. Notice also that just as in the first example, the interpreter could use a specific hand movement for the ending *-ing*. The interpreter may also use other hand movements to indicate other word endings, specifically *-ed* and *-s*. This is sometimes necessary because, as stated before, manual codes are not languages. They are communication systems that follow English rules.

TECHNIQUES In addition to learning languages and codes, interpreters must study the various techniques people use to communicate their ideas and feelings. Mouth and eye movements, facial expressions, and body movements are as important to full communication as vocabulary and grammar. In a spoken language, these devices may add subtle but important meanings to a message, but in ASL they are an integral part of the language itself. For example, when asking a yes/no question, a deaf person raises the eyebrows at the beginning of a sentence. A hearing person raises the pitch of the voice at the end of a sentence. An interpreter must be aware of these important, nonverbal, grammatical elements.

WOOD

Let's look at another example. A deaf person who forms the sign for PIECE OF WOOD uses the lips as well as the hands to show how thick the wood is. In turn, an interpreter must choose the exact English word for the particular piece of wood the signer means. Will it be a twig, a limb, a beam, or a rafter? The interpreter chooses the particular English word but bases the choice on the signer's intention. Thus, it is the interpreter's knowledge in both languages and his or her ability to read and express nonverbal signals that determine how well deaf people and hearing people communicate.

SICK

In a conditional sentence, such as "If Gorby eats petunias, he will get sick," a deaf person does not sign the words *if-then*. Instead, the deaf person will shift the body to one side for the "if" clause, and raise the eyebrows. For the "then" clause the signer will shift the body to the

*An interpreter's work may vary from day
to day. Here it includes interpreting
a speech by Senator Edward Kennedy.*

other side and lower the eyebrows. The interpreter must
let his hearing audience know that a statement is conditional by supplying the missing words. Or, in the reverse,
the interpreter must supply the body motions and facial
expressions that indicate the spoken words "if" and "then."

MODE Another specialized term that interpreters use is the word
mode. Mode refers to the way in which people deliver or
receive messages. A person can hear, speak, sign, see, or
feel a language. We call these five methods *communication modes*. ASL uses a visual/gestural mode. That is, we
can see (visual) the language or sign (gestural) it. Spoken
English uses an aural/oral mode. That is, we can hear (aural)

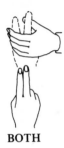

BOTH

the language or speak (oral) it. PSE might use various combinations of these modes: oral, aural, visual, and gestural. People using it might combine speaking, hearing, signing, and seeing. Some sign communication modes also use a tactile mode. People who are both deaf and blind use this method to communicate. The only way they can communicate is by feel.

The tactile mode requires that the message giver form his or her own hands into the required shapes and signs necessary to communicate a message. The message receiver lightly places both hands on the hands of the message giver. It is a tedious way to communicate but, under certain circumstances, the only way possible.

Interpreters help to increase communication between people. They are able to use various languages, modes, and codes to help people understand each other. In order to do this, they must learn many skills and constantly practice using them. Interpreting demands concentration from those involved in the work. The rewards of this profession come from the satisfaction of helping people help themselves and from meeting the challenges of a job that varies from day to day.

CHAPTER 3   WHO DOES WHAT

An interpreter generally works in groups of at least three people: the interpreter, the hearing person, and the hearing-impaired person. The interpreter acts as a *facilitator*. A facilitator is someone who makes the communication process easier between a hearing and a hearing-impaired person. We call the hearing and hearing-impaired people *consumers*. Consumers are the people who use and pay for the services of interpreters.

CONSUMERS' RESPONSIBILITIES

EASY

Everyone who participates in the communication process must take some responsibility for the easy give-and-take of information. With the help of the interpreter, the consumers are responsible for introducing everyone in the group to one another. Consumers also have the responsibility of explaining to all those present the interpreter's role and responsibilities. They do this so that everyone will understand what the interpreter will and will not do.

For example, everyone in the room should know that the interpreter will speak or sign everything that will happen during the communication process. Nothing will be

SECRET

REASON

deleted and no secrets kept. This is important. Hearing-impaired individuals have a right to know everything they might overhear or be told if they were able to hear.

In a medical situation, it becomes the interpreter's responsibility to see to it that the doctor does not discuss any health-related matter with the interpreter while the deaf consumer is not present. Such situations used to happen quite frequently. Well-meaning doctors and "protectors" may have thought it wise to keep information from deaf adults for the same reason that adults sometimes withhold information from children. This lack of information prevented deaf people from making wise and independent decisions. It kept them from being self-reliant. It is the responsibility of the professional interpreter along with the consumer to ensure that this does not happen.

CHOOSING THE PLACE

COLORS

In order for hearing-impaired people to be able to participate fully in the communication process, they must have clear visual contact with all those who are communicating with each other. It is the consumers and the interpreters who decide together exactly where the interpreting will take place. A room may be too dark, too bright, too noisy, or too cluttered for good communication to occur. Hearing-impaired people must rely on their eyes for information, and if they cannot see well or if they are distracted by bright colors on the walls, they will have a hard time participating in the communication. Hearing people depend heavily on their ears, and if they cannot hear well, they will also have a hard time participating in the communication process.

The hearing-impaired person and the interpreter also decide if the interpreter should sit or stand and where the interpreter should sit or stand. Sometimes deaf consumers prefer that the interpreter sit near them rather than near the person who is speaking. This decision is usually a matter of both preference and circumstances. The closer the hearing-impaired person is to the interpreter, the easier it is for him or her to see the face and the mouth of the interpreter.

*An interpreter (right) fluent in both spoken
English and ASL interprets for the hearing
person (center) and the deaf person (left).*

On the other hand, under certain conditions, such as a
theatrical performance or political speech, a deaf person
might prefer that the interpreter stand near the speaker so
that he or she can see the facial expressions of the actors
or the speaker, as well as the face of the interpreter. Circumstances and personal preferences influence the physical
setup of the interpretation.

BEGIN

**INTERPRETERS'
RESPONSIBILITIES**
In addition to being involved in the above details, interpreters have other responsibilities. For example, they must
find out before the interpreting begins what language (i.e.,

The situation and the needs of the consumers
are important factors that influence
where the interpreter stands or sits.

ASL or English), or combination of languages, their consumers prefer to use. They must also know what modes or codes (if any) to use. Most interpreters learn this information by talking informally with their consumers before the interpreting process begins. Sometimes, however, they will ask direct questions about the consumer's language and mode preference. Interpreters need to discover which communication skills will be most effective.

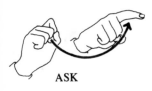

ASK

Interpreters should dress in a way that will not call too much attention to themselves or distract their consumers. (Normally, solid-colored clothing that contrasts with skin color is advised.) Long, brightly painted fingernails, dangling earrings, or unkempt hair may be very distracting to some people. The interpreters must use good judgment and dress appropriately according to the situation. For example, it would be inappropriate to dress the same way for a basketball assignment as for a courtroom assignment.

Finally, a good interpreter will work to achieve the best possible communication environment for consumers. This means that if there is something about the environment that makes communication difficult, the interpreter will ask for it to be changed. Should a light be turned on? Should an air conditioner be turned off or a window or door closed? Perhaps the group would be better off using another room. In order for the communication process to go smoothly, a deaf person needs the best possible light and an interpreter needs the lowest level of auditory distractions. An interpreter who requests changes in the environment is said to be *advocating for communication*. It is the professional attitude of the interpreter that makes being an advocator quite different from being a protector.

CHANGE

CODE OF ETHICS

JOIN

Interpreters must know the Code of Ethics of their profession. The RID Code of Ethics applies to all people who have RID certification, whether or not they are members of RID. Some people take the exams and earn certification, but for reasons of their own never formally join RID. Certified people, however, are obligated to follow the Code of Ethics. If they don't, they may be in danger of losing their national RID certification and may not be allowed to work as professional interpreters.

The Code of Ethics is meant to be a general guide for interpreters. Although not all interpreters need apply the code exactly the same way, they all need to be aware that there is a code, and if they wish to be considered professional, the public will expect certain things of them.

Confidentiality · The Code of Ethics requires confidentiality. This means that interpreters may not give the names of the consumers they are interpreting for, the place in which they are interpreting, or any details about the interpreting situation to others. This information is private. Revealing private information is like telling a secret. If even one person discovers it, the news might embarrass the deaf consumer or hurt him or her in an even more serious way. This is especially true if the law has been broken or if the deaf consumer lied about something. Since the deaf community is very small, even the tiniest bit of revealed information might hurt a hearing-impaired person. Thus, the code requires that the interpreter keep all details of the communication confidential.

Impartiality · Interpreters must be impartial and objective. The code states that even if interpreters are asked for their own personal opinions related to an interpreted situation, they must not give them. For example, if a deaf person is confused about which car to buy, he or she may ask a friend for a personal opinion but not the interpreter. Interpreters should not give advice when they are in the role of an interpreter. The job of an interpreter is to facilitate communication, not to "help."

The difference between the professional role of facilitator and the friendly role of helper is important to note. To act professionally, an interpreter may not offer advice while interpreting, even if the deaf consumer is a good friend or relative. That is one reason why some interpreters do not accept professional interpreting jobs for friends and

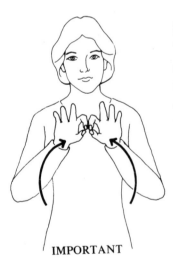

IMPORTANT

At political demonstrations or rallies,
the interpreter is called upon to transmit the
speaker's fervor along with the message.

relatives. They are afraid that they might not be objective. Thus, many interpreters feel it is best to have someone who is not personally involved with the consumer act as the interpreter.

Honesty · Another requirement of the code is honesty. Interpreters are expected to be honest in their transmission of the message. This also means that the interpreter must transmit the message with the intent and mood the message giver expressed. Sometimes this is very difficult. For example, a message giver might use words or signs that embarrass the interpreter. Even when this happens, however, the interpreter must accurately say or sign those words.

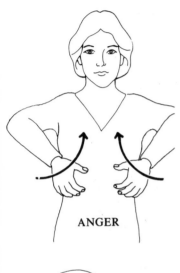

ANGER

Sometimes it is not the ideas that are difficult to transmit but rather the manner in which the consumer expresses those ideas. For example, if the hearing consumer is very angry and this anger is expressed by the volume level of the spoken words, the interpreter must somehow transmit this level of anger. Interpreters must show anger in their choice of signs and facial expression, in their use of body language, and in their speed of transmission. They must show this anger, even when they do not feel it themselves. This is difficult to do and sometimes takes acting skill.

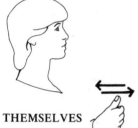

THEMSELVES

In the reverse, the interpreter must also communicate any anger expressed by the hearing-impaired person. To do this, the interpreter must translate the angry signs and loud vocal noises into loud, harsh words. Interpreters may sometimes feel as though the consumers' anger is directed at them rather than at each other. This puts a lot of pressure on the interpreter. However, in order to conform to the code, the interpreter must communicate the mood and language of the message givers. It is the responsibility of the interpreter to make certain that everyone understands the true feelings in the situation.

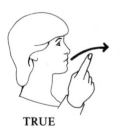

TRUE

Discretion · Interpreters must also use discretion regarding their own skill level and choice of assignment. This means that interpreters should not accept assignments in situations where they do not feel qualified or comfortable. Just as an eye doctor (opthalmologist) will refuse to set broken bones

HOSPITAL

WEDDING

BEFORE

and a skin doctor (dermatologist) won't prescribe contact lenses, so a particular interpreter may not feel qualified to handle all interpreting situations. Some interpreters, for example, may not feel comfortable working in a jail cell. They may be afraid. Their nervousness will show and act as a barrier to the smooth flow of communication. These people should not accept a jail assignment.

Others may not feel at ease in a hospital setting. Certain religious situations might also be difficult for some interpreters. For example, it is quite possible that a Jewish interpreter might feel uncomfortable interpreting at a Catholic wedding, especially if the rites of the ceremony are unfamiliar to him or her. If this is the case, the Jewish interpreter would be using discretion by refusing the job. In other words, the code expects interpreters to refuse assignments as paid professionals in situations where they do not feel at ease or lack the skill level. It is up to the individuals to decide for themselves what assignments to accept and what assignments to refuse. No one expects all interpreters to have the same level of communication skills or to be comfortable in every situation.

Other Professional Matters · Payment for work done is another area the Code of Ethics covers. It states that interpreters should always expect to be paid in some way for their services. If the consumer does not offer to pay, the interpreter should ask for a fee. The interpreter should request this compensation before the interpreting process begins. The compensation does not always have to be in the form of money.

If the interpreter knows that a consumer cannot afford to pay for the interpreter's services, then the interpreter can decide what form the pay will take. A dinner invitation or the performance of a favor can be substituted for cash payment. The issue of compensation is an important one, and it is the interpreter's responsibility to see that all details concerning it are settled beforehand.

Finally, the Code of Ethics provides guidelines in an area called *professionality*. Professionality concerns two subjects: behavior and professional participation. In matters dealing with behavior, the code encourages interpreters to be polite and pleasant to all people with whom they work. It states that interpreters ought to dress in a professional manner. In addition, the guidelines discourage interpreters from doing anything that might draw attention to themselves or distract their consumers in any way.

On the subject of professional participation, the code recognizes the importance of interpreters making ongoing efforts to increase their knowledge, improve their skills, and keep up-to-date with changes within the interpreting field. Therefore, the code encourages interpreters to be constantly involved in learning.

Most professional interpreters willingly apply these guidelines to their work. The result has been that consumers, both hearing and hearing impaired, have increased their respect for the special work of interpreters.

CHAPTER 4 WHERE AND HOW

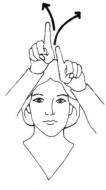

STAR

Interpreters can work anyplace. They are called to commencements when deaf students graduate or when hearing students with deaf parents want them to know what is going on during the ceremonies. They may work at ballparks so that deaf people can participate in the singing of "The Star-Spangled Banner." They may work with foreign-language interpreters during group tours in foreign nations. They may attend plays and school with their deaf clients and be there when the hearing impaired have appointments with doctors, lawyers, and counselors.

Interpreters have a chance to learn about and participate in every area of life because the hearing-impaired people they serve participate in every area of life. Interpreters may act very much like shadows, following hearing-impaired individuals around in their jobs or at school.

As in most professions, interpreters can specialize. A specialist is a person who has general skills in an overall field but special skills in a certain aspect of that field. For example, a pediatrician is a doctor. He or she specializes in medicine for children. A psychiatrist is also a doctor, but he or she specializes in the diagnosis and treatment of mental disorders. Interpreters, too, have specialties. For each kind of specialization, the interpreter must become familiar with the unique vocabulary and techniques needed to interpret in that special setting.

THEATRICAL INTERPRETERS

HOUR

Theatrical interpreters, for example, must use large signs so that the audience can see the interpretation clearly. Like the actors in the play, they must spend many hours rehearsing the play they will interpret. In addition, they must always be ready for the unexpected. For example, in one particular theatrical production, there was an interpreter onstage interpreting during a sword fight. The actors became rather energetic, and to avoid being stabbed the interpreter had to duck occasionally and nimbly shift her stage position several times during the performance.

Theatrical interpreters don't always work onstage. Sometimes they are off to the side or just below the stage. Usually they have a light shining on them so that the hearing impaired in the audience can see their facial expressions and body movements. There are times, however, when technicians may fail to turn back on the interpreter's spotlight after intermission. Nevertheless, the show and the interpreting must go on. Sometimes it is possible for the interpreter to move his or her chair out of a shadow in order to become visible to the hearing impaired in the audience. Imagination and good judgment help.

Far more hearing-impaired children and adults enjoy the theater today because of sign-language interpreters. When an interpreter is present, they can understand what is happening instead of trying to guess.

EDUCATIONAL INTERPRETERS

Educational interpreters are the largest and fastest-growing group of interpreters in the United States today. They work in elementary schools, high schools, technical schools, and colleges. The main reason there are so many educational interpreters today is because of certain federal laws.

With the help of a sign language interpreter,
a group of deaf children can enjoy a performance
of the opera, The Merry Wives of Windsor.

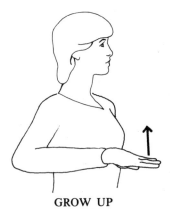

GROW UP

ROOM

For example, if a hearing-impaired child can benefit from attending school with hearing children, then by federal law the school district in which the child lives must provide this opportunity. The idea of handicapped children going to school with children who are not handicapped is called *mainstreaming*. It gives everyone a chance to learn about everyone else.

In a mainstreamed classroom, hearing children and deaf children learn how to communicate with one another. They also learn about the different cultures in which they live. Often this mainstreaming leads to greater understanding among people. Many people believe that when children in mainstreamed classrooms grow up, they will be more likely to respect differences among all people than children who have grown up only with people like themselves.

Sometimes it is scary when a hearing-impaired student and his or her interpreter enter a regular classroom for the first time. The teacher may feel uncomfortable with an extra adult always in the room. The hearing students may also feel ill at ease because they do not know how to communicate with this new person. At first, no one knows what to expect. Teachers may even blame the interpreter for these difficulties.

Once things settle down, though, an interpreter can be a great help to everyone. For example, the interpreter can act as an extra aide in the classroom. He or she can also assist a hearing student and a hearing-impaired student to communicate with each other so that they can become friends. In time, the two friends may be able to communicate without the aid of the interpreter.

The laws about mainstreaming are not the only laws that affect the interpreting profession. Section 504 of the Vocational Rehabilitation Act of 1973, mentioned earlier, also affects it. The law states that any program, institution, or place of employment that accepts money from the federal government must promise to make it possible for handicapped people to learn, work, or take advantage of the services it offers.

At a union conference on issues affecting the deaf and hearing impaired, an interpreter ensures that deaf participants can follow the proceedings.

For hearing-impaired individuals, this usually means hiring an interpreter. Before the federal government passed these laws, the hearing impaired did not receive many of the services they needed. Instead they became frustrated and unhappy because they could not understand what was happening around them. The law changed their lives. Communication is much easier when there is an interpreter around. It is unfortunate, though, that there is still a huge shortage of educational interpreters.

POLICE

WRONG

Interpreters also work in police stations and with lawyers. When a deaf person is involved in a crime, as a victim, witness, or perpetrator, an interpreter is often needed to explain the situation to the deaf person. Legal interpreters make certain that the words of the police, lawyers, and judge are conveyed correctly to the deaf person.

Interpreters who work in legal settings have a big responsibility. They must make very certain that ideas are conveyed back and forth in a way that the deaf person fully understands. If this does not happen, the deaf person may not have a chance to give his or her side of the story. This would be especially serious if the deaf person is either the individual accused of a wrongdoing or the one accusing someone else.

Sometimes a defense lawyer will hire a second interpreter to make certain that the court-appointed interpreter is correctly interpreting the testimony of a deaf witness. This is especially true if the deaf person's statements are extremely important to the outcome of the trial.

Some interpreters might find the assignment of checking up on another interpreter quite difficult. It could easily happen that one interpreter must publicly call attention to the mistakes another interpreter makes. To publicly criticize a person in one's own profession is usually considered unprofessional. That's why doctors and teachers, for example, don't usually criticize one another in front of others. However, the seriousness of the situation may require such evaluations.

Interpreters in legal settings must be very skilled. Sometimes it is necessary for the interpreter to get special training in the legal system. These interpreters learn the special vocabulary and procedures used in legal settings.

**HEALTH-CARE
INTERPRETERS**

Interpreters can work in a variety of jobs within the health-care industry. These jobs might range from interpreting at drug rehabilitation centers to interpreting in emergency rooms or in surgery. Like educational and legal interpreting, the law requires health-care interpreting. Deaf individuals have a right to know all the information the health-care providers can give them regarding their health. Deaf people, just like hearing people, need this information in order to make intelligent decisions about their own lives and bodies.

NURSE

Interpreters in health-care situations make it easier for deaf individuals to relate their medical history to doctors, nurses, and technicians. They also ease the process of explaining medical risks and surgical procedures. With an interpreter present, both the hearing-impaired consumer and the health-care professional may ask questions and give answers. As a result, there is greater understanding and less fear.

In the future, interpreters in health-care settings will probably work as members of a team. That is, each deaf patient will have a single health-care interpreter in much the same way that each patient has his or her own physician. The reason for this is that when a health-care interpreter is involved with a patient for a long time, that interpreter comes to know many details about the patient's life and illness. With a single health-care interpreter, a caring relationship can grow in much the same way as the caring relationship between doctor and patient.

WAY

Health-care interpreting, like other specialty interpreting, requires knowledge of a specialized vocabulary. Although the health-care personnel must take the responsibility of explaining new terminology to the patient, the interpreter's job is easier if he or she knows medical vocabulary and procedures.

At the moment, St. Mary's Campus of the College of St. Catherine in St. Paul, Minnesota, is the only school in the country that trains health-care interpreters. At the end of a two-year program, these very specialized interpreters can easily get jobs in medical settings. Not all health-care interpreters attend this specialized training program. Instead they learn their skills by watching other interpreters and attending workshops and classes.

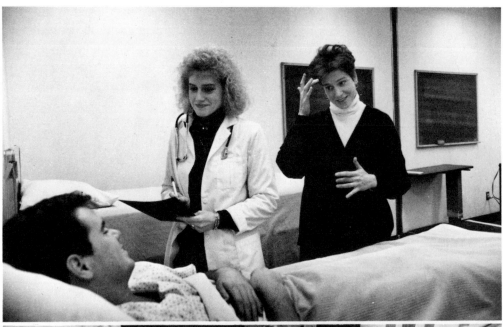

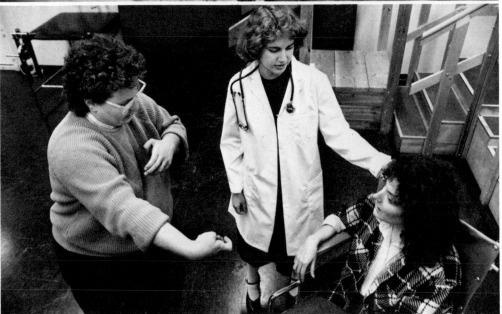

*Health-care interpreting students at St. Mary's
Campus of the College of St. Catherine practice
bedside interpreting skills (top) and interpreting
in a physical therapy session (bottom).*

MENTAL-HEALTH INTERPRETERS

The mental-health area is a specialty within the health-care area. As in the other medical specialties, mental-health interpreters use a specialized vocabulary and may work as part of a medical team. Mental-health interpreters interpret in therapy sessions. Therapy is a process whereby clients with the help of a therapist learn to understand themselves. Therapists generally talk with clients to get them to understand why they act the way they do. When necessary a therapist will help a client to change his or her behavior patterns.

Interpreters have a very challenging job in the mental-health setting. They must pay careful attention to the language both the therapist and client use and transmit faithfully any information the hearing-impaired person reveals, so that the therapist can use this information as a tool for change.

Not many interpreters feel qualified to work in the mental-health area. They feel that they need a great deal of experience before they can successfully convey all of the words, feelings, and hidden meanings of language. Those interpreters who do feel qualified work with individuals, groups, and entire families.

EXPERIENCE

THE WORKING WORLD

Another area of specialization is related to the working world. Interpreters work in places where hearing-impaired clients train for future employment. Because of certain laws, disabled people receive special help first as they train for employment and then later as they seek employment. Interpreters make the step-by-step process from training to interview to job placement easier. Sometimes interpreters start a new job along with the hearing-impaired consumer. However, as soon as the hearing-impaired individual gains enough confidence to work without an interpreter, the interpreter leaves.

Both hearing people and deaf people are getting used to having interpreters around. Anyone can hire an interpreter. A couple about to get married might hire an interpreter

This interpreter enables the deaf and hearing impaired to participate in religious services.

TELEPHONE

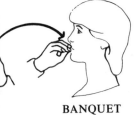

BANQUET

either because they want to understand the vows they are going to take or because the parents or guests of either the bride or groom are hearing impaired and the couple wants them all to feel a part of the festivities. A hearing-impaired college president or business executive might hire an interpreter to help him or her talk on the telephone, conduct interviews, travel, or attend a meeting. A travel agent might hire an interpreter and so might a person planning a banquet. The problem for an interpreter working at a banquet is that frequently the interpreter does not have the opportunity to eat. Interpreters cannot sign when their hands are busy any better than people can speak when their mouths are full!

The role of the interpreter is to enable the hearing impaired to communicate as easily as possible in a hearing world. The hearing world is a large one, and therefore the career opportunities for interpreters are many.

For more information about testing and the interpreting profession, write to:

RID, Inc. (Registry of Interpreting for the Deaf)
51 Monroe
Suite 1107
Rockville, MD 20850

For information on deafness write to:

NAD (National Association of the Deaf)
814 Thayer Avenue
Silver Spring, MD 20910

NICD (National Information Center on Deafness)
Gallaudet University
800 Florida Avenue, NE
Washington, DC 20002

CHAPTER 5 TRAINING, EVALUATION, AND CERTIFICATION

DOCTOR

INTELLIGENT

There are many ways to become an interpreter. Some people enter the profession by studying interpreting and earning a degree at a four-year or two-year college. Others become interpreters by attending classes and workshops sponsored by a private agency. A few people become interpreters simply through the trial-and-error method of on-the-job experience.

In the past, there was little agreement on exactly what skills and what knowledge interpreters needed. No one required that interpreters be licensed to practice the way doctors, lawyers, and teachers must be licensed in order to practice their professions. Professional licenses usually require that the holder take a particular course of study, achieve certain skills, and demonstrate these skills before an examining board. Before the famous Ball State conference (see Chapter One), all people had to do to call themselves interpreters was to interpret.

The result of this was that people who called themselves interpreters were often unqualified. Well-meaning but unskilled people sometimes interpreted incorrectly. It often appeared that hearing-impaired people were less intelligent than hearing people.

MEETING (NOUN)

All of this changed as a result of the Indiana meeting. RID began by establishing a set of standards and then proceeded to raise these standards as necessary. This development from setting standards to improving standards has helped make interpreting a respected profession.

RID has worked hard to educate the public about the necessity of having and enforcing standards. Certified interpreters now work in almost every area in which people communicate: medicine, law, politics, entertainment, education, and so on. The quality of their work has allowed the hearing and nonhearing communities to relate to one another on a much more nearly equal basis.

Today the demand for certified interpreters is greater than the supply. This is both good and bad—good because it means that people finally recognize the many ways interpreters can help; and bad because since there aren't enough certified interpreters, people with insufficient skills are still able to work as interpreters. RID is working to change this.

RID The evaluation section of RID is composed of two parts. One part, the National Certification Board (NCB), sets the standards people must meet in order to become certified interpreters. These standards relate not only to their skills in translating one language into another, but also to the candidates' professional behavior and ethics. The NCB has the power to revoke certification if a person wrongfully interprets or violates the RID Code of Ethics.

The second section, the National Evaluation Board (NEB), designs the tests leading to certification. Over the last several years, there have been a number of different types of certifications. Some were for hearing people only. Some were for the hearing impaired only.

The requirements in each certification category ranged from considerable proficiency in a large number of different skills to certificates that required less proficiency and fewer skills. There were also special certifications for people who wished to work in theatrical or legal settings. Fi-

With the assistance of an interpreter (left), a deaf person can serve as a member of a jury.

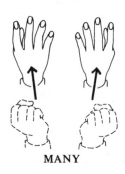

MANY

nally, RID offered a variety of oral-interpretation certificates. Many people felt that oral-interpretation certifications were necessary because there are some hearing-impaired people who use speech and speech reading as their major form of communication. These people do not know sign language and rely primarily on lipreading. In addition, although they speak English, their speech is not always understood by hearing people. These English-speaking deaf people sometimes need oral interpreters to facilitate communication.

Videotape cameras are an instruction tool at an interpreting class. The interpreter-trainer (behind camera) tapes a student (right) signing to a trainer (center).

WRITE

An oral interpreter, for example, might attend a lecture with a hearing-impaired person. The interpreter will sit facing the hearing-impaired individual and mouth the words of the speaker. This is necessary because frequently a lecturer moves back and forth while talking or turns away to write on the chalkboard. The hearing-impaired person is then unable to see the speaker's mouth.

RID helped develop standards for oral skills. Those who demonstrated these skills could earn an oral-interpretation certificate. One certificate indicated the ability to paraphrase the spoken message of a hearing person and put this message into the speech and mouth movements a hearing-impaired person could understand. Another certificate indicated the ability to translate the speech and mouth movement of a deaf person into the sounds that a hearing person could understand. A third certificate indicated that the interpreter was able to translate both spoken English to visual English and visual English to spoken.

Recently, the NCB and NEB revised the entire certification system. It is no longer possible to earn RID certification in oral interpreting. The Alexander Graham Bell Association, an organization that encourages oral communication for the deaf, is the only organization that offers certification for oral interpreters. Although most hearing-impaired people use a form of sign language as their major form of communication, some hearing-impaired people require the services of oral interpreters, particularly at public presentations.

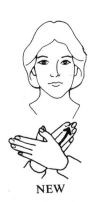

NEW

The new RID system now offers only two kinds of certification. One is for interpreting. The other is for transliterating. People who earn either or both of these certifications must demonstrate considerable skills in various areas, including ASL, spoken English, and manual codes for English.

As of April 1988, candidates for either certification must pass a written test before they may take the performance portion. The written test is a two-part multiple-choice examination. The first part deals with ethical standards, and the second part deals with knowledge of the profession and the deaf community. All of the tests are standardized. This means that all candidates, no matter where they live, take the same test.

The performance test requires that the candidate demonstrate an acceptable ability in either interpreting or transliterating. It has five separate parts and requires that the candidates watch five videotapes and then interpret them for evaluators while being videotaped themselves. Evaluators rate the videotapes at a later time. Applicants must interpret three particular tapes but may choose among several alternatives for the other two.

To earn the Interpreting Certification (IC), a person must be able to change ASL into spoken English and the reverse. Candidates for the Transliteration Certificate (TC) must be able to work between spoken English and manual codes for English.

Three evaluators look at the videotapes of the candidate's performance and independently of one another decide whether the person has passed. The evaluators are one deaf person, one hearing person, and one interpreter. To become an evaluator, a person must pass an Evaluator Selection test. However, even after a person passes this test, the NCB, NEB, and NES (National Evaluation System) will continue to monitor the skills and decision-making ability of the evaluators.

SUMMER

RID administered the first written test of this new system in the spring of 1988. Of the 112 applicants who took the test, 66 passed. The first performance test was given in the summer of 1988.

It has been RID's policy for many years to publish the names of those who pass the certification tests. This policy will continue, as will RID's effort to distribute this list to anyone who needs it.

BECOMING CERTIFIED

Since it takes many years to become a certified sign language interpreter, most interpreters are adults. Children with deaf parents and children who know sign language well are encouraged to think about sign language interpreting as a career. For more information get in touch with your state RID chapter.

At the present time, if a person wants to become a certified interpreter, all he or she needs to do is to pass the tests. It does not matter how old the person is or how that person acquired interpreting or transliterating skills. What does matter is the person's ability to demonstrate specific skills in a testing situation. It is the evaluators who determine who will receive RID certification.

The NCB charges a fee for those who wish to take the test. There is an additional fee for the official RID *NES Study Guide.* The publication is about thirty pages long and contains information and suggestions for preparing for the test. It includes a copy of the Code of Ethics and sample questions. By reading *RID Views,* the organization's newsletter, interested people can find out which test site is nearest their home. The tests are given several times a year in various places in both the United States and Canada.

Some potential interpreters do not choose to go through RID testing as a first step. Instead they begin with a screening and evaluation program designed to assess their interpreting and sign-language skills. This program is called the Quality Assurance Testing System (QA), and it enables individuals to determine where their strengths and weaknesses are. Later, they may decide to earn RID certification.

The designers of the QA program established it for evaluation purposes only. The people in the various states and regions who write the questions regulate the quality of the tests. Recently, some state agencies, organizations, and institutions who do not understand the RID system have been hiring people who have received only their QA results. They mistakenly believe this is the same as RID certification. As a result, there are interpreters with minimal skills working in jobs for which they are not qualified. In some states, levels of pay are dependent upon levels of QA and RID certification.

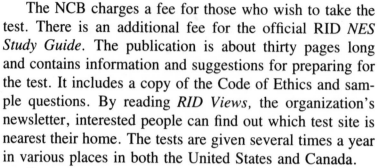

CANADA

PROFESSIONAL ORGANIZATIONS

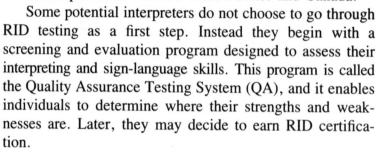

Every profession has at least one organization that allows its members to communicate with one another and share information and ideas. Some organizations may be international, such as the International Association of Approved Basketball Officials or the International Association of Ice Cream Manufacturers. Others may be national, such

CHEWING GUM

as the American Medical Association, or the National Association of Chewing Gum Manufacturers. Some are even statewide, such as the Council for Wisconsin Writers. The point is that every profession needs an organization to enable people with a particular interest to keep up-to-date in their field.

Sign language interpreters are no exception. You already know about one national organization: RID, Inc., and its two parts, the NCB and NEB. RID also has state chapters. Although not every state has a RID chapter, some have two. RID affiliates go by different acronyms, such as WISRID (Wisconsin RID) or NORCRID (Northern California RID).

In addition to RID and its affiliates, other organizations that might be useful to sign interpreters are the National Association of the Deaf, American Deafness and Rehabilitation Association, Sign Instructors Guidance Network (SIGN), Conference of Interpreter Trainers (CIT), and various state associations of the deaf.

THE FUTURE

SCHOOL

The present RID certification system has changed quite a bit in recent years. It is likely to change again. Someday, for example, people may have to formally study interpreting in school before they can qualify for the test. Some states may require licenses. Specialty certificates may one day be available again. The only thing we can predict for sure is that things will change. However, from now on, interpreters will more and more be professionally qualified people who competently serve the needs of the hearing impaired by assisting them to communicate in a hearing world.

CHAPTER 6 PRACTICE TIME

Now it's time to practice some of your new signing skills. The first thing an interpreter must do is decide on the important ideas that must be put into American Sign Language. The second thing is to arrange those ideas to fit into the grammar of ASL. Only after this is done does an interpreter begin to sign. Here is an example of the process.

Pretend for a moment that you are a hearing person and you want to tell your deaf friend about your coming birthday party. Suppose this is what you want to say:

GAMES

Next week I will have a *birthday party*. It will be a *big celebration*. We will *play games*. We will *search* for *silly things*. The really *special* thing we will do is *ride* in a *helicopter*. My *sister wants us* to *fly far* away, but I do *not like* that *idea*. We *should* be *home* by *midnight*.

The italicized words are the main ideas. They are listed on the next page.

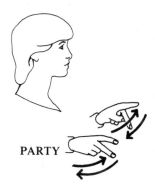

PARTY

Major Ideas:
next week birthday party
big celebration
play games
search silly things
special ride helicopter
sister wants us fly far
do not like idea
should home midnight

BIG

Now put these ideas into ASL order. Usually the topic is first, the comment is second, and the time reference is last. The topic is what we want to talk about. The comment is what we want to say about it, and the time is when the action took place or will take place.

In our above example, the paragraph breaks down like this:

TOPIC	COMMENT	TIME
party	birthday	next week
celebration	big	
games	play	
silly things	search	
special helicopter	ride	
sister wants us	fly far	
idea	not like	
home	should	midnight

PARAGRAPH

Finally, it is signed:

BIRTHDAY

TIME

NEXT WEEK

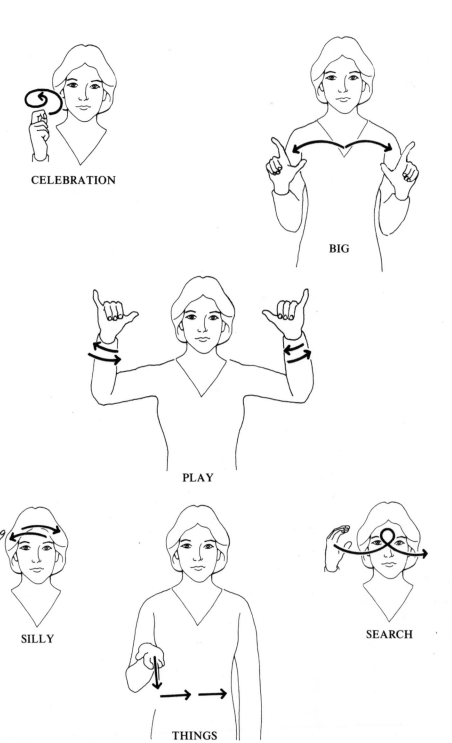

CELEBRATION

BIG

PLAY

SILLY

THINGS

SEARCH

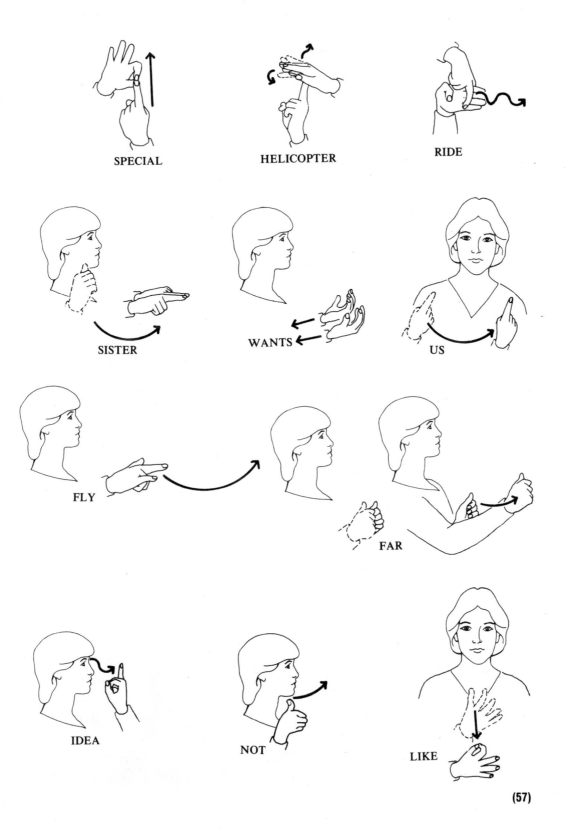

SPECIAL HELICOPTER RIDE

SISTER WANTS US

FLY FAR

IDEA NOT LIKE

(57)

HOME

SHOULD

MIDNIGHT

TIME

This time, try it by yourself. First look at each paragraph below. Think of the main ideas. It helps to write them down. Now arrange the ideas into three columns: TOPIC, COMMENT, and TIME. Check your answers below, and then, with the help of the dictionary following this chapter, see if you can sign the statements.

EXERCISE #1
SHARING NEWS
WITH A DEAF
FRIEND

My mother and father are not home yet. They are visiting my brother. He is in the hospital. Last week my brother and his roommate were in a car accident. They will go home next week.

EXERCISE #2
INVITING
A FRIEND TO SHARE
NEW PAINTS

Can you come to my house next week? Maybe we can use my new art supplies. I have different kinds of paper and all sorts of paints. The two of us will make funny masks.

EXERCISE #3
A DREAM

STRANGE

A long time ago I had a silly dream. I saw my brother far away from me. He was sitting on the roof of a house. He was reading from sheets of paper. Then a strange thing happened. My father sat with my brother on the roof. Together they began reading from the paper. It seemed as if they were acting in a play.

(58)

THE ANSWERS **Exercise #1**
Sharing News with a Deaf Friend

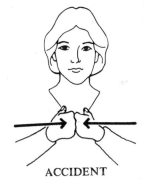

ACCIDENT

My *mother* and *father* are *not home yet*. *They* are *visiting* my *brother*. *He* is in the *hospital*. *Last week my brother and* his *roommate* were in a *car accident*. *They* will *go home next week*.

Major Ideas:

mother, father, not home yet
they visit my brother
he hospital
last week my brother and roommate car accident
they go home next week

TOPIC	COMMENT	TIME
mother, father	home	not yet
my brother	they visit	
He (brother)	hospital	
my brother and roommate	car accident	last week
home	they go	next week

Now turn to the dictionary for the correct signs.

WILL

Exercise #2
Inviting a Friend to Share New Paints

Can *you come* to *my house next week*? Maybe we can *use* my *new art supplies*. I *have different* kinds of *paper* and all sorts of *paints*. The *two of us will make funny masks*.

Major Ideas:

you, come, my house, next week?
use, new, art supplies
have, different, paper, paints
two of us, will, make, funny, masks

TOPIC	COMMENT	TIME
house, my	you come	next week
new, art supplies	use	
paper, paints	have different	
masks, funny	two-of-us, make	will

(59)

Now turn to the dictionary for the correct signs.

Exercise #3
A Dream

A long time ago I had a *silly dream. I saw my brother far away* from me. He was *sitting* on the *roof* of a *house. He* was *reading* from sheets of *paper.* Then a *strange* thing *happened. My father sat with* my *brother* on the *roof.* Together *they* began *reading* from the *paper. It seemed* as if *they* were acting in a *play.*

SITTING

Major Ideas:
A long time ago, I, silly dream
saw my brother far away
sitting, roof, house
He reading paper
strange happened
father sat with brother roof
they reading paper
seemed they play

TOPIC	COMMENT	TIME
I dream	silly	a long time ago
brother, my	far away	
sitting	house, roof	
paper	he, read	
happened	strange	
brother, father	sat-together, roof	
paper	they read	
seemed, they	play	

Now turn to the dictionary for the correct signs.

THE MANUAL ALPHABET

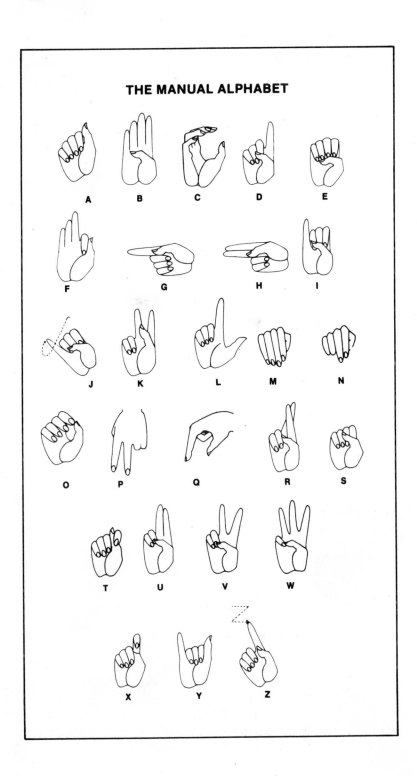

DICTIONARY

A (article)
"A" position moves to side.

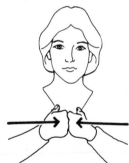

ACCIDENT Fists come together.
Back of hands touch.

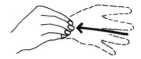

AND   Open hand moves as fingers come together.

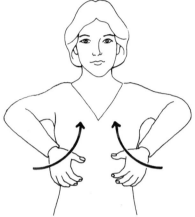

ANGER   Bent fingers touch ribs and move
upward in fast motion.

ASK   Index finger thrusts out as it moves from a closed fist.

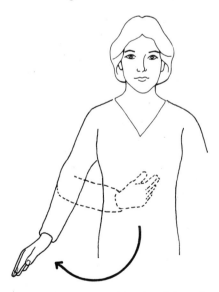

AWAY   Natural gesture. Back of hand pushes away from body.

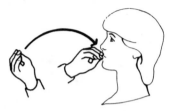

BANQUET   Closed fingers on both hands.
Move hands toward mouth alternately.

BEFORE   Right and left palms face in.
Right hand moves toward body.

BEGIN   Right index finger twists clockwise between fingers.

BIG   "L" position on both hands,
palms facing each other.
Hands move out.

BIRTHDAY (birth and day)
(birth) Right hand, palm in,
moves toward left hand, palm in.
(day) "D" position on right hand.
Right elbow touches left fingertips
and moves down to left elbow.

BLIND Bent "V" position is held under eyes.

BOAT Sides of hands touching.
Hand moves forward in wavy motion.

BOTH Right "V" position moves
down through "C" position on
left hand, fingers closing.

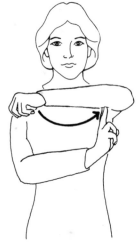

BRIDGE ''V'' position on right hand
moves from wrist to elbow under
left arm.

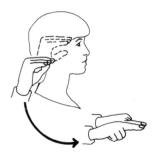

BROTHER Closed ''O'' position touches
forehead and moves to touch left
and right index fingers together.

CANADA Right fist grasps right lapel.

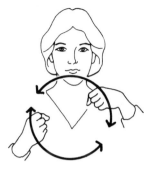

CAR   Fists hold imaginary steering
wheel and turn back and forth.

CELEBRATION   Closed "X" position circles in air.

CHANGE   Left and right wrists face each other.
Hands twist to opposite position.

CHEWING GUM   Two fingers on right hand touch
lower right cheek and rock in and out.

COLOR   Fingers wiggle in front of mouth.

COME   Open palm gestures toward body.

DAY   ''D'' position on right hand.
Right elbow touches left fingertips
and moves down to left elbow.

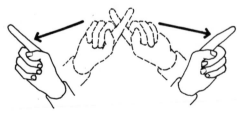

DIFFERENT   Palms facing down.
Index fingers move apart.

DOCTOR   Hand with "D" position taps lightly on left wrist.

DREAM   Index finger moves away from forehead as "X" position wiggles up and down.

EASY   Side of right hand brushes tips of left hand in upward motion.

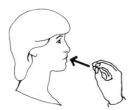

EAT   Closed "O" position touches mouth.

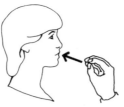

EATING   From Eat position, "I" position twists so palm faces out.

EXPERIENCE Tips of hand touch temple
and move down, closing fingers.

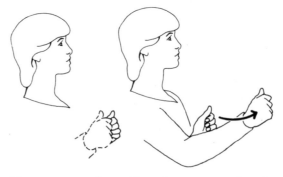

FAR Fists are together. One fist moves ahead.

FATHER Closed ''O'' position touches forehead
and opens hands, palms up.

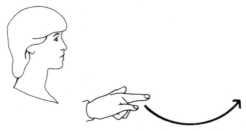

FLY Thumb, index finger, and little finger move in space.

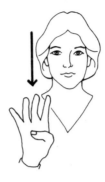

FOUR Four fingers held upright.

FUNNY Two fingers brush down across nose.

GAME ''A'' position on both hands.
Knuckles come together and move up.

GO Index fingers on both
hands arc forward.

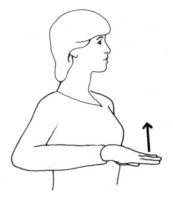

GROW UP Right hand, palm down,
slowly moves up.

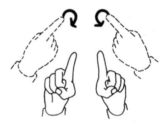

HAPPEN Index fingers extended on both hands,
palms facing up. Turn hands quickly
so palms face down.

HAVE Tips of both hands touch chest.

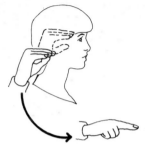

HE   Index finger points.

HELICOPTER   Index finger tip held in upright position
against palm of other hand.

HOME   Closed "O" position touches mouth and side of cheek.

HOSPITAL   "H" position on right hand makes
cross emblem on left upper arm.

HOUR Left hand held upright, palm facing right. Right index finger makes complete circle against palm.

HOUSE Fingertips touch and move down at an angle like the roof of a house.

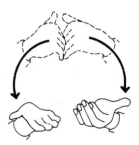

HOW Backs of fingers touch each other and turn, ending with palms up.

I (PRONOUN) Small finger brought against chest.

IDEA "I" position moves away from head.

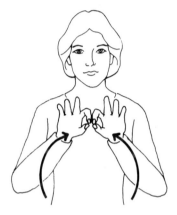

IMPORTANT "F" positions on both hands. Hands move up and together, thumb tips touching.

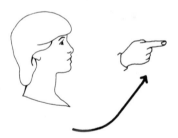

INDEX Pointing to an imaginary person or thing is called "indexing."

-ing "I" position twists so palm faces out.

INTELLIGENT Index finger moves away from forehead.

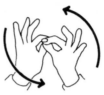

INTERPRET Both hands in "F" position.
Thumb tips touch and alternate
in back-and-forth movement.

IS Small finger in "I" position moves
straight out from mouth.

JOIN Two fingers on right hand are put into left fist.

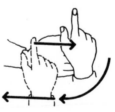

LAST WEEK Right index finger points up.
Right palm touches left palm,
moves to right and moves back of signer.

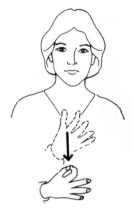

LIKE Thumb and index finger touch chest
and move away, touching fingertips.

LOOK AT ''V'' position on right hand twists from
eye position, palm facing out.

LONG AGO Hand with open palm moves over shoulder.

MAKE Place one fist on top of the other.
Twist wrists in alternating motion.

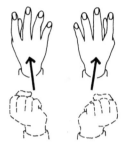

MANY   Fists on both hands open as hands move up.

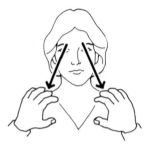

MASK   "C" position hands with fingers spread move down the face.

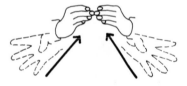

MEETING   Open hands face each other and move upward. Fingers close as fingertips touch.

MIDNIGHT   Right hand points straight down, left hand touches elbow.

MONEY   Closed "O" position on right hand.
Back of right hand rests in open left palm.

MOTHER   "A" position hand touches cheek
and opens hand, palm up.

MY   Open palm rests on chest.

NEW   Both palms face body. Back of
right palm moves up against left palm.

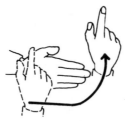

NEXT WEEK   Palms face each other. Right index finger up.
Moves across left palm and up.

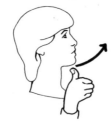

NOT   Thumb moves out from under chin.

NOT YET   Right hand hangs down. Palm faces back.
Wrist pushes hand back once or more.

NURSE   Right hand places two fingers on left wrist at pulse.

ON   Right hand rests on left hand. Palms face down.

ONE   Index finger held up.

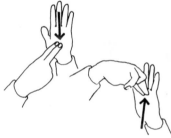

PAINT   Two fingers of right hand brush up and down.

PAPER   Palms face each other. Top hand brushes
bottom hand in same direction.

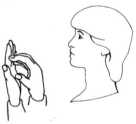

PARAGRAPH   Right hand "C" position
rests on open palm on left hand,
fingertips touch palm.

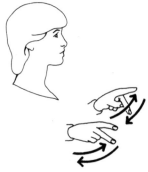

PARTY "P" positions on both hands.
Wrists move in back-and-forth motion.

PLAY Both hands with "Y" position.
Wrists move back and forth.

PAST (in time)
Hand with open palm
moves over shoulder.

POLICE   Right hand is held against chest in ''C'' position.

PRACTICE   ''A'' position on right hand brushes extended index finger on left hand.

PRIDE   Hand in ''A'' position moves upward in middle of chest. Thumb held against chest.

READ Two fingers on right hand move down open palm of left hand.

REASON ''R'' position on right hand circles center of forehead.

RIDE ''V'' position on right hand placed over side of left hand. Both hands move ahead.

ROOF Right hand moves in downward motion from under left hand.

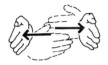

ROOM   Palms face each other. Both move to perpendicular positions and face each other.

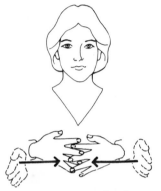

ROOMMATE   Palms face in. Fingers on both hands interlock.

SAT TOGETHER   Bent ''V'' position on both hands move together.

SCHOOL   Hands clap together.

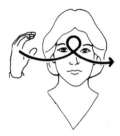

SEARCH   Right hand with a "C" position loops
across face from right to left.

SECRET   "A" position hand
touches mouth.

SEEM   Right palm faces left, wrist twists
back and forth.

SHOULD   "X" position moves down,
fingertips facing floor.

SICK   Longest finger on right hand taps forehead. Longest finger on left hand taps stomach.

SILLY   "Y" position on right hand moves back and forth across face. Palm faces left.

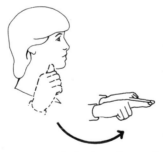

SISTER   "A" position on right hand touches right cheek and moves to touch left and right index fingers together.

SITTING   Two fingers of one hand rest on two fingers of other hand.

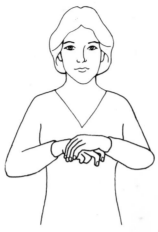

SNAIL Right hand cups top of left hand.
Two fingers stick out,
resembling snail antennae.

SPECIAL Left thumb and index finger pull
right index finger up.

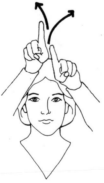

STAR Index fingers brush past each
other, alternately, moving up.

STRANGE ''C'' position on right hand moves across face from right to left.

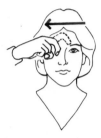

SUMMER Right hand ''X'' position moves across forehead.

SUPPLY Right hand moves across body to the right, palm up.

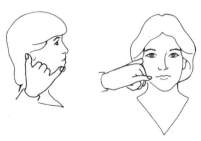

TELEPHONE Right hand holds ''Y'' position at the ear. Thumb touches ear and small finger reaches mouth.

TEN Thumb shakes back and forth.

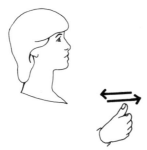

THEMSELVES ''A'' position makes slight back-and-forth motions.

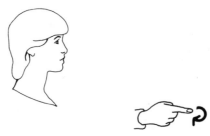

THEY Index finger circles to indicate people or things.

THING Right hand moves across body to the right, palm up.

THINK   Index finger makes small circle on corner of forehead.

THREE   Two fingers and thumb held upright.

TIME   ''T'' position on right hand moves in circular motion against left palm.

TRUE   Index finger tip touches mouth and arcs up and out.

TWO OF US   ''V'' position moves between signer and other person.

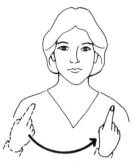

US   Right index finger touches right chest
and arcs to left chest.

USE   ''U'' position circles in air.

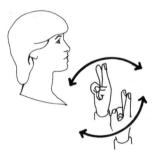

VISIT   ''V'' position circles alternately.

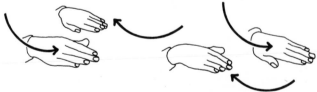

WALK   Hands flat with palms down. Hands alternately
move forward and backward.

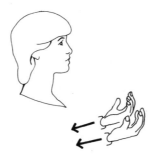

WANT "C" position on both hands, palms up.
Hands move toward body.

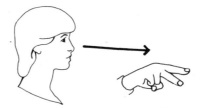

WATCH "V" position on right hand points ahead, palm down.

WAY Both hands in "W" positions move ahead in
wiggling manner. Palms face each other.

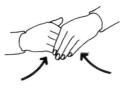

WEDDING Right hand moves under left hand.
Left thumb grasps right hand.

WHEN Right index finger circles tip of left index finger.

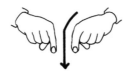

WHILE　Index fingers move forward in parallel line.

WHO　Index finger circles mouth counterclockwise.

WILL　Right hand moves forward on side of right cheek.

WOOD　Bottom of right hand moves back and forth in sawing motion on back of left hand. Left palm faces down.

WRITE　Right hand with closed fingers moves across left palm in writing motion.

WRONG   Hand in "Y" position rests on bottom of chin.

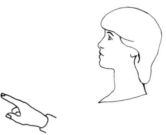

YOU   Point to person.

INDEX